THE NATIONAL SECURITY STRATEGY

OF THE UNITED STATES OF AMERICA

MARCH 2006

My fellow Americans,

America is at war. This is a wartime national security strategy required by the grave challenge we face – the rise of terrorism fueled by an aggressive ideology of hatred and murder, fully revealed to the American people on September 11, 2001. This strategy reflects our most solemn obligation: to protect the security of the American people.

America also has an unprecedented opportunity to lay the foundations for future peace. The ideals that have inspired our history – freedom, democracy, and human dignity – are increasingly inspiring individuals and nations throughout the world. And because free nations tend toward peace, the advance of liberty will make America more secure.

These inseparable priorities – fighting and winning the war on terror and promoting freedom as the alternative to tyranny and despair – have now guided American policy for more than 4 years.

We have kept on the offensive against terrorist networks, leaving our enemy weakened, but not yet defeated.

We have joined with the Afghan people to bring down the Taliban regime – the protectors of the al-Qaida network – and aided a new, democratic government to rise in its place.

We have focused the attention of the world on the proliferation of dangerous weapons – although great challenges in this area remain.

We have stood for the spread of democracy in the broader Middle East – meeting challenges yet seeing progress few would have predicted or expected.

We have cultivated stable and cooperative relations with all the major powers of the world.

We have dramatically expanded our efforts to encourage economic development and the hope it brings – and focused these efforts on the promotion of reform and achievement of results.

We led an international coalition to topple the dictator of Iraq, who had brutalized his own people, terrorized his region, defied the international community, and sought and used weapons of mass destruction.

And we are fighting alongside Iraqis to secure a united, stable, and democratic Iraq – a new ally in the war on terror in the heart of the Middle East.

We have seen great accomplishments, confronted new challenges, and refined our approach as conditions changed. We have also found that the defense of freedom brings us loss and sorrow, because freedom has determined enemies. We have always known that the war on terror would require great sacrifice – and in this war, we have said farewell to some very good men and women. The terrorists have used dramatic acts of murder – from the streets of Fallujah to the subways of London – in an attempt to undermine our will. The struggle against this enemy – an enemy that targets the innocent without conscience or hesitation – has been difficult. And our work is far from over.

America now faces a choice between the path of fear and the path of confidence. The path of fear – isolationism and protectionism, retreat and retrenchment – appeals to those who find our challenges too great and fail to see our opportunities. Yet history teaches that every time American leaders have taken this path, the challenges have only increased and the missed opportunities have left future generations less secure.

This Administration has chosen the path of confidence. We choose leadership over isolationism, and the pursuit of free and fair trade and open markets over protectionism. We choose to deal with challenges now rather than leaving them for future generations. We fight our enemies abroad instead of waiting for them to arrive in our country. We seek to shape the world, not merely be shaped by it; to influence events for the better instead of being at their mercy.

The path we have chosen is consistent with the great tradition of American foreign policy. Like the policies of Harry Truman and Ronald Reagan, our approach is idealistic about our national goals, and realistic about the means to achieve them.

To follow this path, we must maintain and expand our national strength so we can deal with threats and challenges before they can damage our people or our interests. We must maintain a military without peer – yet our strength is not founded on force of arms alone. It also rests on economic prosperity and a vibrant democracy. And it rests on strong alliances, friendships, and international institutions, which enable us to promote freedom, prosperity, and peace in common purpose with others.

Our national security strategy is founded upon two pillars:

The first pillar is promoting freedom, justice, and human dignity – working to end tyranny, to promote effective democracies, and to extend prosperity through free and fair trade and wise development policies. Free governments are accountable to their people, govern their territory effectively, and pursue economic and political policies that benefit their citizens. Free governments do not oppress their people or attack other free nations. Peace and international stability are most reliably built on a foundation of freedom.

The second pillar of our strategy is confronting the challenges of our time by leading a growing community of democracies. Many of the problems we face – from the threat of pandemic disease, to proliferation of weapons of mass destruction, to terrorism, to human trafficking, to natural disasters – reach across borders. Effective multinational efforts are essential to solve these problems. Yet history has shown that only when we do our part will others do theirs. America must continue to lead.

GEORGE W. BUSH
THE WHITE HOUSE
March 16, 2006

TABLE OF CONTENTS

I.   Overview of America's National Security Strategy

It is the policy of the United States to seek and support democratic movements and institutions in every nation and culture, with the ultimate goal of ending tyranny in our world. In the world today, the fundamental character of regimes matters as much as the distribution of power among them. The goal of our statecraft is to help create a world of democratic, well-governed states that can meet the needs of their citizens and conduct themselves responsibly in the international system. This is the best way to provide enduring security for the American people.

Achieving this goal is the work of generations. The United States is in the early years of a long struggle, similar to what our country faced in the early years of the Cold War. The 20th century witnessed the triumph of freedom over the threats of fascism and communism. Yet a new totalitarian ideology now threatens, an ideology grounded not in secular philosophy but in the perversion of a proud religion. Its content may be different from the ideologies of the last century, but its means are similar: intolerance, murder, terror, enslavement, and repression.

Like those who came before us, we must lay the foundations and build the institutions that our country needs to meet the challenges we face. The chapters that follow will focus on several essential tasks. The United States must:

- Champion aspirations for human dignity;

- Strengthen alliances to defeat global terrorism and work to prevent attacks against us and our friends;

- Work with others to defuse regional conflicts;

- Prevent our enemies from threatening us, our allies, and our friends with weapons of mass destruction (WMD);

- Ignite a new era of global economic growth through free markets and free trade;

- Expand the circle of development by opening societies and building the infrastructure of democracy;

- Develop agendas for cooperative action with other main centers of global power;

- Transform America's national security institutions to meet the challenges and opportunities of the 21st century; and

- Engage the opportunities and confront the challenges of globalization.

II.   Champion Aspirations for Human Dignity

A. Summary of National Security Strategy 2002

The United States must defend liberty and justice because these principles are right and true for all people everywhere. These nonnegotiable demands of human dignity are protected most securely in democracies. The United States Government will work to advance human dignity in word and deed, speaking out for freedom and against violations of human rights and allocating appropriate resources to advance these ideals.

B. Successes and Challenges since 2002

Since 2002, the world has seen extraordinary progress in the expansion of freedom, democracy, and human dignity:

- The peoples of Afghanistan and Iraq have replaced tyrannies with democracies.

  - In Afghanistan, the tyranny of the Taliban has been replaced by a freely-elected government; Afghans have written and ratified a constitution guaranteeing rights and freedoms unprecedented in their history; and an elected legislature gives the people a regular voice in their government.

  - In Iraq, a tyrant has been toppled; over 8 million Iraqis voted in the nation's first free and fair election; a freely negotiated constitution was passed by a referendum in which almost 10 million Iraqis participated; and, for the first time in their history, nearly 12 million Iraqis have elected a permanent government under a popularly determined constitution.

- The people of Lebanon have rejected the heavy hand of foreign rule. The people of Egypt have experienced more open but still flawed elections. Saudi Arabia has taken some preliminary steps to give its citizens more of a voice in their government. Jordan has made progress in opening its political process. Kuwait and Morocco are pursuing agendas of political reform.

- The "color revolutions" in Georgia, Ukraine, and Kyrgyzstan have brought new hope for freedom across the Eurasian landmass.

- Democracy has made further advances in Africa, Latin America, and Asia, with peaceful transfers of power; growth in independent judiciaries and the rule of law; improved election practices; and expanding political and economic rights.

The human desire for freedom is universal, but the growth of freedom is not inevitable. Without support from free nations, freedom's spread could be hampered by the challenges we face:

- Many governments are at fragile stages of political development and need to consolidate democratic institutions – and leaders that have won democratic elections need to uphold the principles of democracy;

- Some governments have regressed, eroding the democratic freedoms their peoples enjoy;

- Some governments have not delivered the benefits of effective democracy and prosperity to their citizens, leaving them susceptible to or taken over by demagogues peddling an anti-free market authoritarianism;

- Some regimes seek to separate economic liberty from political liberty, pursuing prosperity while denying their people basic rights and freedoms; and

- Tyranny persists in its harshest form in a number of nations.

C. The Way Ahead

The United States has long championed freedom because doing so reflects our values and advances our interests. It reflects our values because we believe the desire for freedom lives in every human heart and the imperative of human dignity transcends all nations and cultures.

Championing freedom advances our interests because the survival of liberty at home increasingly depends on the success of liberty abroad. Governments that honor their citizens' dignity and desire for freedom tend to uphold responsible conduct toward other nations, while governments that brutalize their people also threaten the peace and stability of other nations. Because democracies are the most responsible members of the international system, promoting democracy is the most effective long-term measure for strengthening international stability; reducing regional conflicts; countering terrorism and terror-supporting extremism; and extending peace and prosperity.

To protect our Nation and honor our values, the United States seeks to extend freedom across the globe by leading an international effort to end tyranny and to promote effective democracy.

1. Explaining the Goal: Ending Tyranny

Tyranny is the combination of brutality, poverty, instability, corruption, and suffering, forged under the rule of despots and despotic systems. People living in nations such as the Democratic People's Republic of Korea (DPRK), Iran, Syria, Cuba, Belarus, Burma, and Zimbabwe know firsthand the meaning of tyranny; it is the bleak reality they endure every day. And the nations they border know the consequences of tyranny as well, for the misrule of tyrants at home leads to instability abroad. All tyrannies threaten the world's interest in freedom's expansion, and some tyrannies, in their pursuit of WMD or sponsorship of terrorism, threaten our immediate security interests as well.

Tyranny is not inevitable, and recent history reveals the arc of the tyrant's fate. The 20th century has been called the "Democracy Century," as tyrannies fell one by one and democracies rose in their stead. At mid-century about two dozen of the world's governments were democratic; 50 years later this number was over 120. The democratic revolution has embraced all cultures and all continents.

Though tyranny has few advocates, it needs more adversaries. In today's world, no tyrant's rule can survive without the support or at least the tolerance of other nations. To end tyranny we must summon the collective outrage of the free world against the oppression, abuse, and impoverishment that tyrannical regimes inflict on their people – and summon their collective action against the dangers tyrants pose to the security of the world.

An end to tyranny will not mark an end to all global ills. Disputes, disease, disorder, poverty, and injustice will outlast tyranny, confronting democracies long after the last tyrant has fallen. Yet tyranny must not be tolerated – it is a crime of man, not a fact of nature.

2. Explaining the Goal: Promoting Effective Democracies

As tyrannies give way, we must help newly free nations build effective democracies: states that are respectful of human dignity, accountable to their citizens, and responsible towards their neighbors. Effective democracies:

- Honor and uphold basic human rights, including freedom of religion, conscience, speech, assembly, association, and press;

- Are responsive to their citizens, submitting to the will of the people, especially when people vote to change their government;

- Exercise effective sovereignty and maintain order within their own borders, protect independent and impartial systems of justice, punish crime, embrace the rule of law, and resist corruption; and

- Limit the reach of government, protecting the institutions of civil society, including the family, religious communities, voluntary associations, private property, independent business, and a market economy.

In effective democracies, freedom is indivisible. Political, religious, and economic liberty advance together and reinforce each other. Some regimes have opened their economies while trying to restrict political or religious freedoms. This will not work. Over time, as people gain control over their economic lives, they will insist on more control over their political and personal lives as well. Yet political progress can be jeopardized if economic progress does not keep pace. We will harness the tools of economic assistance, development aid, trade, and good governance to help ensure that new democracies are not burdened with economic stagnation or endemic corruption.

Elections are the most visible sign of a free society and can play a critical role in advancing effective democracy. But elections alone are not enough – they must be reinforced by other values, rights, and institutions to bring about lasting freedom. Our goal is human liberty protected by democratic institutions.

Participation in elections by individuals or parties must include their commitment to the equality of all citizens; minority rights; civil liberties; voluntary and peaceful transfer of power; and the peaceful resolution of differences. Effective democracy also requires institutions that can protect individual liberty and ensure that the government is responsive and accountable to its citizens. There must be an independent media to inform the public and facilitate the free exchange of ideas. There must be political associations and political parties that can freely compete. Rule of law must be reinforced by an independent judiciary, a professional legal establishment, and an honest and competent police force.

These principles are tested by the victory of Hamas candidates in the recent elections in the Palestinian territories. The Palestinian people voted in a process that was free, fair, and inclusive.

The Palestinian people having made their choice at the polls, the burden now shifts to those whom they have elected to take the steps necessary to advance peace, prosperity, and statehood for the Palestinian people. Hamas has been designated as a terrorist organization by the United States and European Union (EU) because it has embraced terrorism and deliberately killed innocent civilians. The international community has made clear that there is a fundamental contradiction between armed group and militia activities and the building of a democratic state. The international community has also made clear that a two-state solution to the conflict requires all participants in the democratic process to renounce violence and terror, accept Israel's right to exist, and disarm as outlined in the Roadmap. These requirements are clear, firm, and of long standing. The opportunity for peace and statehood – a consistent goal of this Administration – is open if Hamas will abandon its terrorist roots and change its relationship with Israel.

The elected Hamas representatives also have an opportunity and a responsibility to uphold the principles of democratic government, including protection of minority rights and basic freedoms and a commitment to a recurring, free, and fair electoral process. By respecting these principles, the new Palestinian leaders can demonstrate their own commitment to freedom and help bring a lasting democracy to the Palestinian territories. But any elected government that refuses to honor these principles cannot be considered fully democratic, however it may have taken office.

3. How We Will Advance Freedom: Principled in Goals and Pragmatic in Means

We have a responsibility to promote human freedom. Yet freedom cannot be imposed; it must be chosen. The form that freedom and democracy take in any land will reflect the history, culture, and habits unique to its people.

The United States will stand with and support advocates of freedom in every land. Though our principles are consistent, our tactics will vary. They will reflect, in part, where each government is on the path from tyranny to democracy. In some cases, we will take vocal and visible steps on behalf of immediate change. In other cases, we will lend more quiet support to lay the foundation for future reforms. As we consider which approaches to take, we will be guided by what will most effectively advance freedom's cause while we balance other interests that are also vital to the security and well-being of the American people.

In the cause of ending tyranny and promoting effective democracy, we will employ the full array of political, economic, diplomatic, and other tools at our disposal, including:

- Speaking out against abuses of human rights;

- Supporting publicly democratic reformers in repressive nations, including by holding high-level meetings with them at the White House, Department of State, and U.S. Embassies;

- Using foreign assistance to support the development of free and fair elections, rule of law, civil society, human rights, women's rights, free media, and religious freedom;

- Tailoring assistance and training of military forces to support civilian control of the military and military respect for human rights in a democratic society;

- Applying sanctions that designed to target those who rule oppressive regimes while sparing the people;

- Encouraging other nations not to support oppressive regimes;

- Partnering with other democratic nations to promote freedom, democracy, and human rights in specific countries and regions;

- Strengthening and building new initiatives such as the Broader Middle East and North Africa Initiative's Foundation for the Future, the Community of Democracies, and the United Nations Democracy Fund;

- Forming creative partnerships with nongovernmental organizations and other civil society voices to support and reinforce their work;

- Working with existing international institutions such as the United Nations and regional organizations such as the Organization for Security and Cooperation in Europe, the African Union (AU), and the Organization of American States (OAS) to help implement their democratic commitments, and helping establish democracy charters in regions that lack them;

- Supporting condemnation in multilateral institutions of egregious violations of human rights and freedoms;

- Encouraging foreign direct investment in and foreign assistance to countries where there is a commitment to the rule of law, fighting corruption, and democratic accountability; and

- Concluding free trade agreements (FTAs) that encourage countries to enhance the rule of law, fight corruption, and further democratic accountability.

These tools must be used vigorously to protect the freedoms that face particular peril around the world: religious freedom, women's rights, and freedom for men, women, and children caught in the cruel network of human trafficking.

- Against a terrorist enemy that is defined by religious intolerance, we defend the First Freedom: the right of people to believe and worship according to the dictates of their own conscience, free from the coercion of the state, the coercion of the majority, or the coercion of a minority that wants to dictate what others must believe.

- No nation can be free if half its population is oppressed and denied fundamental rights. We affirm the inherent dignity and worth of women, and support vigorously their full participation in all aspects of society.

- Trafficking in persons is a form of modern-day slavery, and we strive for its total abolition. Future generations will not excuse those who turn a blind eye to it.

Our commitment to the promotion of freedom is a commitment to walk alongside governments and their people as they make the difficult transition to effective democracies. We will not abandon them before the transition is secure because immature democracies can be prone to conflict and vulnerable to exploitation by terrorists. We will not let the challenges of democratic transitions frighten us into clinging to the illusory stability of the authoritarian.

America's closest alliances and friendships are with countries with whom we share common values and principles. The more countries demonstrate that they treat their own citizens with respect and are committed to democratic principles, the closer and stronger their relationship with America is likely to be.

The United States will lead and calls on other nations to join us in a common international effort. All free nations have a responsibility to stand together for freedom because all free nations share an interest in freedom's advance.

III. **Strengthen Alliances to Defeat Global Terrorism and Work to Prevent Attacks Against Us and Our Friends**

A. **Summary of National Security Strategy 2002**

Defeating terrorism requires a long-term strategy and a break with old patterns. We are fighting a new enemy with global reach. The United States can no longer simply rely on deterrence to keep the terrorists at bay or defensive measures to thwart them at the last moment. The fight must be taken to the enemy, to keep them on the run. To succeed in our own efforts, we need the support and concerted action of friends and allies. We must join with others to deny the terrorists what they need to survive: safe haven, financial support, and the support and protection that certain nation-states historically have given them.

B. **Current Context: Successes and Challenges**

The war against terror is not over. America is safer, but not yet safe. As the enemy adjusts to our successes, so too must we adjust. The successes are many:

- Al-Qaida has lost its safe haven in Afghanistan.

- A multinational coalition joined by the Iraqis is aggressively prosecuting the war against the terrorists in Iraq.

- The al-Qaida network has been significantly degraded. Most of those in the al-Qaida network responsible for the September 11 attacks, including the plot's mastermind Khalid Shaykh Muhammad, have been captured or killed.

- There is a broad and growing global consensus that the deliberate killing of innocents is never justified by any calling or cause.

- Many nations have rallied to fight terrorism, with unprecedented cooperation on law enforcement, intelligence, military, and diplomatic activity.

- Numerous countries that were part of the problem before September 11 are now increasingly becoming part of the solution – and this transformation has occurred without destabilizing friendly regimes in key regions.

- The Administration has worked with Congress to adopt and implement key reforms like the Patriot Act which promote our security while also protecting our fundamental liberties.

The enemy is determined, however, and we face some old and new challenges:

- Terrorist networks today are more dispersed and less centralized. They are more reliant on smaller cells inspired by a common ideology and less directed by a central command structure.

- While the United States Government and its allies have thwarted many attacks, we have not been able to stop them all. The terrorists have struck in many places, including Afghanistan, Egypt, Indonesia, Iraq, Israel, Jordan, Morocco, Pakistan, Russia, Saudi Arabia, Spain, and the United Kingdom. And they continue to seek WMD in order to inflict even more catastrophic attacks on us and our friends and allies.

- The ongoing fight in Iraq has been twisted by terrorist propaganda as a rallying cry.

- Some states, such as Syria and Iran, continue to harbor terrorists at home and sponsor terrorist activity abroad.

C. The Way Ahead

From the beginning, the War on Terror has been both a battle of arms and a battle of ideas – a fight against the terrorists and against their murderous ideology. In the short run, the fight involves using military force and other instruments of national power to kill or capture the terrorists, deny them safe haven or control of any nation; prevent them from gaining access to WMD; and cut off their sources of support. In the long run, winning the war on terror means winning the battle of ideas, for it is ideas that can turn the disenchanted into murderers willing to kill innocent victims.

While the War on Terror is a battle of ideas, it is not a battle of religions. The transnational terrorists confronting us today exploit the proud religion of Islam to serve a violent political vision: the establishment, by terrorism and subversion, of a totalitarian empire that denies all political and religious freedom. These terrorists distort the idea of jihad into a call for murder against those they regard as apostates or unbelievers – including Christians, Jews, Hindus, other religious traditions, and all Muslims who disagree with them. Indeed, most of the terrorist attacks since September 11 have occurred in Muslim countries – and most of the victims have been Muslims.

To wage this battle of ideas effectively, we must be clear-eyed about what does and does not give rise to terrorism:

- Terrorism is not the inevitable by-product of poverty. Many of the September 11 hijackers were from middle-class backgrounds, and many terrorist leaders, like bin Laden, are from privileged upbringings.

- Terrorism is not simply a result of hostility to U.S. policy in Iraq. The United States was attacked on September 11 and earlier, well before we toppled the Saddam Hussein regime. Moreover, countries that stayed out of the Iraq war have not been spared from terror attack.

- Terrorism is not simply a result of Israeli-Palestinian issues. Al-Qaida plotting for the September 11 attacks began in the 1990s, during an active period in the peace process.

- Terrorism is not simply a response to our efforts to prevent terror attacks. The al-Qaida network targeted the United States long before the United States targeted al-Qaida. Indeed, the terrorists are emboldened more by perceptions of weakness than by demonstrations of resolve. Terrorists lure recruits by telling them that we are decadent and easily intimidated and will retreat if attacked.

The terrorism we confront today springs from:

- Political alienation. Transnational terrorists are recruited from people who have no voice in their own government and see no legitimate way to promote change in their own country. Without a stake in the existing order, they are vulnerable to manipulation by those who advocate a perverse vision based on violence and destruction.

- Grievances that can be blamed on others. The failures the terrorists feel and see are blamed on others, and on perceived injustices from the recent or sometimes distant past. The terrorists' rhetoric keeps wounds associated with this past fresh and raw, a potent motivation for revenge and terror.

- Sub-cultures of conspiracy and misinformation. Terrorists recruit more effectively from populations whose information about the world is contaminated by falsehoods and corrupted by conspiracy theories. The distortions keep alive grievances and filter out facts that would challenge popular prejudices and self-serving propaganda.

- An ideology that justifies murder. Terrorism ultimately depends upon the appeal of an ideology that excuses or even glorifies the deliberate killing of innocents. A proud religion – the religion of Islam – has been twisted and made to serve an evil end, as in other times and places other religions have been similarly abused.

Defeating terrorism in the long run requires that each of these factors be addressed. The genius of democracy is that it provides a counter to each.

- In place of alienation, democracy offers an ownership stake in society, a chance to shape one's own future.

- In place of festering grievances, democracy offers the rule of law, the peaceful resolution of disputes, and the habits of advancing interests through compromise.

- In place of a culture of conspiracy and misinformation, democracy offers freedom of speech, independent media, and the marketplace of ideas, which can expose and discredit falsehoods, prejudices, and dishonest propaganda.

- In place of an ideology that justifies murder, democracy offers a respect for human dignity that abhors the deliberate targeting of innocent civilians.

Democracy is the opposite of terrorist tyranny, which is why the terrorists denounce it and are willing to kill the innocent to stop it. Democracy is based on empowerment, while the terrorists' ideology is based on enslavement. Democracies expand the freedom of their citizens, while the terrorists seek to impose a single set of narrow beliefs. Democracy sees individuals as equal in worth and dignity, having an inherent potential to create and to govern themselves. The terrorists see individuals as objects to be exploited, and then to be ruled and oppressed.

Democracies are not immune to terrorism. In some democracies, some ethnic or religious groups are unable or unwilling to grasp the benefits of freedom otherwise available in the society. Such groups can evidence the same alienation and despair that the transnational terrorists exploit in undemocratic states. This accounts for the emergence in democratic societies of homegrown terrorists such as were responsible for the bombings in London in July 2005 and for the violence in some other nations. Even in these cases, the long-term solution remains deepening the reach of democracy so that all citizens enjoy its benefits.

The strategy to counter the lies behind the terrorists' ideology is to empower the very people the terrorists most want to exploit: the faithful followers of Islam. We will continue to support political reforms that empower peaceful Muslims to practice and interpret their faith. The most vital work will be done within the Islamic world itself, and Jordan, Morocco, and Indonesia have begun to make important strides in this effort. Responsible Islamic leaders need to denounce an ideology that distorts and exploits Islam for destructive ends and defiles a proud religion.

Many of the Muslim faith are already making this commitment at great personal risk. They realize they are a target of this ideology of terror. Everywhere we have joined in the fight against terrorism, Muslim allies have stood beside us, becoming partners in this vital cause. Pakistan and Saudi Arabia have launched effective efforts to capture or kill the leadership of the al-Qaida network. Afghan troops are in combat against Taliban remnants. Iraqi soldiers are sacrificing to defeat al-Qaida in their own country. These brave citizens know the stakes – the survival of their own liberty, the future of their own region, the justice and humanity of their own traditions – and the United States is proud to stand beside them.

The advance of freedom and human dignity through democracy is the long-term solution to the transnational terrorism of today. To create the space and time for that long-term solution to take root, there are four steps we will take in the short term.

- **Prevent attacks by terrorist networks before they occur.** A government has no higher obligation than to protect the lives and livelihoods of its citizens. The hard core of the terrorists cannot be deterred or reformed; they must be tracked down, killed, or captured. They must be cut off from the network of individuals and institutions on which they depend for support. That network must in turn be deterred, disrupted, and disabled by using a broad range of tools.

- **Deny WMD to rogue states and to terrorist allies who would use them without hesitation**. Terrorists have a perverse moral code that glorifies deliberately targeting innocent civilians. Terrorists try to inflict as many casualties as possible and seek WMD to this end. Denying terrorists WMD will require new tools and new international approaches. We are working with partner nations to improve security at vulnerable nuclear sites worldwide and bolster the ability of states to detect, disrupt, and respond to terrorist activity involving WMD.

- **Deny terrorist groups the support and sanctuary of rogue states.** The United States and its allies in the War on Terror make no distinction between those who commit acts of terror and those who support and harbor them, because they are equally guilty of murder. Any government that chooses to be an ally of terror, such as Syria or Iran, has chosen to be an enemy of freedom, justice, and peace. The world must hold those regimes to account.

- **Deny the terrorists control of any nation that they would use as a base and launching pad for terror.** The terrorists' goal is to overthrow a rising democracy; claim a strategic country as a haven for terror; destabilize the Middle East; and strike America and other free nations with ever-increasing violence. This we can never allow. This is why success in Afghanistan and Iraq is vital, and why we must prevent terrorists from exploiting ungoverned areas.

America will lead in this fight, and we will continue to partner with allies and will recruit new friends to join the battle.

Afghanistan and Iraq: The Front Lines in the War on Terror

Winning the War on Terror requires winning the battles in Afghanistan and Iraq.

In Afghanistan, the successes already won must be consolidated. A few years ago, Afghanistan was condemned to a pre-modern nightmare. Now it has held two successful free elections and is a staunch ally in the war on terror. Much work remains, however, and the Afghan people deserve the support of the United States and the entire international community.

The terrorists today see Iraq as the central front of their fight against the United States. They want to defeat America in Iraq and force us to abandon our allies before a stable democratic government has been established that can provide for its own security. The terrorists believe they would then have proven that the United States is a waning power and an unreliable friend. In the chaos of a broken Iraq the terrorists believe they would be able to establish a safe haven

---

like they had in Afghanistan, only this time in the heart of a geopolitically vital region. Surrendering to the terrorists would likewise hand them a powerful recruiting tool: the perception that they are the vanguard of history.

When the Iraqi Government, supported by the Coalition, defeats the terrorists, terrorism will be dealt a critical blow. We will have broken one of al-Qaida's most formidable factions – the network headed by Zarqawi – and denied him the safe haven he seeks in Iraq. And the success of democracy in Iraq will be a launching pad for freedom's success throughout a region that for decades has been a source of instability and stagnation.

The Administration has explained in some detail the strategy for helping the Iraqi people defeat the terrorists and neutralize the insurgency in Iraq. This requires supporting the Iraqi people in integrating activity along three broad tracks:

Political: Work with Iraqis to:

- **Isolate** hardened enemy elements who are unwilling to accept a peaceful political process;

- **Engage** those outside the political process who are willing to turn away from violence and invite them into that process; and

- **Build** stable, pluralistic, and effective national institutions that can protect the interests of all Iraqis.

Security: Work with Iraqi Security Forces to:

- **Clear** areas of enemy control by remaining on the offensive, killing and capturing enemy fighters, and denying them safe haven;

- **Hold** areas freed from enemy control with an adequate Iraqi security force presence that ensures these areas remain under the control of a peaceful Iraqi Government; and

- **Build** Iraqi Security Forces and the capacity of local institutions to deliver services, advance the rule of law, and nurture civil society.

Economic: Work with the Iraqi Government to:

- **Restore** Iraq's neglected infrastructure so that Iraqis can meet increasing demand and the needs of a growing economy;

- **Reform** Iraq's economy so that it can be self-sustaining based on market principles; and

- **Build** the capacity of Iraqi institutions to maintain their infrastructure, rejoin the international economic community, and improve the general welfare and prosperity of all Iraqis.

IV. Work with Others to Defuse Regional Conflicts

A. Summary of National Security Strategy 2002

Regional conflicts are a bitter legacy from previous decades that continue to affect our national security interests today. Regional conflicts do not stay isolated for long and often spread or devolve into humanitarian tragedy or anarchy. Outside parties can exploit them to further other ends, much as al-Qaida exploited the civil war in Afghanistan. This means that even if the United States does not have a direct stake in a particular conflict, our interests are likely to be affected over time. Outsiders generally cannot impose solutions on parties that are not ready to embrace them, but outsiders can sometimes help create the conditions under which the parties themselves can take effective action.

B. Current Context: Successes and Challenges

The world has seen remarkable progress on a number of the most difficult regional conflicts that destroyed millions of lives over decades.

- In Sudan, the United States led international negotiations that peacefully resolved the 20-year conflict between the Government of Sudan and the Sudanese Peoples Liberation Movement.

- In Liberia, the United States led international efforts to restore peace and bolster stability after vicious internal conflict.

- Israeli forces have withdrawn from the Gaza Strip and the northern West Bank, creating the prospect for transforming Israeli-Palestinian relations and underscoring the need for the Palestinian Authority to stand up an effective, responsible government.

- Relations between India and Pakistan have improved, with an exchange of high-level visits and a new spirit of cooperation in the dispute over Kashmir – a cooperation made more tangible by humanitarian actions undertaken following a destructive earthquake.

- The cooperative approach to the relief effort following the tsunami that hit Indonesia resulted in political shifts that helped make possible a peaceful settlement in the bitter separatist conflict in Aceh.

- In Northern Ireland, the implementation of key parts of the Good Friday Agreement, including the decommissioning of weapons, marked a substantial milestone in ending that long-standing civil conflict.

Numerous remaining regional challenges demand the world's attention:

- In Darfur, the people of an impoverished region are the victims of genocide arising from a civil war that pits a murderous militia, backed by the Sudanese Government, against a collection of rebel groups.

- In Colombia, a democratic ally is fighting the persistent assaults of Marxist terrorists and drug-traffickers.

- In Venezuela, a demagogue awash in oil money is undermining democracy and seeking to destabilize the region.

- In Cuba, an anti-American dictator continues to oppress his people and seeks to subvert freedom in the region.

- In Uganda, a barbaric rebel cult – the Lord's Resistance Army – is exploiting a regional conflict and terrorizing a vulnerable population.

- In Ethiopia and Eritrea, a festering border dispute threatens to erupt yet again into open war.

- In Nepal, a vicious Maoist insurgency continues to terrorize the population while the government retreats from democracy.

C. The Way Ahead

Regional conflicts can arise from a wide variety of causes, including poor governance, external aggression, competing claims, internal revolt, tribal rivalries, and ethnic or religious hatreds. If left unaddressed, however, these different causes lead to the same ends: failed states, humanitarian disasters, and ungoverned areas that can become safe havens for terrorists.

The Administration's strategy for addressing regional conflicts includes three levels of engagement: conflict prevention and resolution; conflict intervention; and post-conflict stabilization and reconstruction.

Effective international cooperation on these efforts is dependent on capable partners. To this end, Congress has enacted new authorities that will permit the United States to train and equip our foreign partners in a more timely and effective manner. Working with Congress, we will continue to pursue foreign assistance reforms that allow the President to draw on the skills of agencies across the United States Government.

1. Conflict Prevention and Resolution

The most effective long-term measure for conflict prevention and resolution is the promotion of democracy. Effective democracies may still have disputes, but they are equipped to resolve their differences peacefully, either bilaterally or by working with other regional states or international institutions.

In the short term, however, a timely offer by free nations of "good offices" or outside assistance can sometimes prevent conflict or help resolve conflict once started. Such early measures can prevent problems from becoming crises and crises from becoming wars. The United States is ready to play this role when appropriate. Even with outside help, however, there is no substitute for bold and effective local leadership.

Progress in the short term may also depend upon the stances of key regional actors. The most effective way to address a problem within one country may be by addressing the wider regional context. This regional approach has particular application to Israeli-Palestinian issues, the conflicts in the Great Lakes region of Africa, and the conflict within Nepal.

2. Conflict Intervention

Some conflicts pose such a grave threat to our broader interests and values that conflict intervention may be needed to restore peace and stability. Recent experience has underscored that the international community does not have enough high-quality military forces trained and capable of performing these peace operations. The Administration has recognized this need and is working with the North Atlantic Treaty Organization (NATO) to improve the capacity of states to intervene in conflict situations. We launched the Global Peace Operations Initiative at the 2004 G-8 Summit to train peacekeepers for duty in Africa. We are also supporting United Nations (U.N.) reform to improve its ability to carry out peacekeeping missions with enhanced accountability, oversight, and results-based management practices.

3. Post-Conflict Stabilization and Reconstruction

Once peace has been restored, the hard work of post-conflict stabilization and reconstruction must begin. Military involvement may be necessary to stop a bloody conflict, but peace and stability will last only if follow-on efforts to restore order and rebuild are successful. The world has found through bitter experience that success often depends on the early establishment of strong local institutions such as effective police forces and a functioning justice and penal system. This governance capacity is critical to establishing the rule of law and a free market economy, which provide long-term stability and prosperity.

To develop these capabilities, the Administration established a new office in the Department of State, the Office of the Coordinator for Reconstruction and Stabilization, to plan and execute civilian stabilization and reconstruction efforts. The office draws on all agencies of the government and integrates its activities with our military's efforts. The office will also coordinate United States Government efforts with other governments building similar capabilities (such as the United Kingdom, Canada, the EU, and others), as well as with new international efforts such as the U.N. Peacebuilding Commission.

4. Genocide

Patient efforts to end conflicts should not be mistaken for tolerance of the intolerable. Genocide is the intent to destroy in whole or in part a national, ethnic, racial, or religious group. The world needs to start honoring a principle that many believe has lost its force in parts of the international community in recent years: genocide must not be tolerated.

It is a moral imperative that states take action to prevent and punish genocide. History teaches that sometimes other states will not act unless America does its part. We must refine United States Government efforts – economic, diplomatic, and law-enforcement – so that they target those individuals responsible for genocide and not the innocent citizens they rule. Where perpetrators of mass killing defy all attempts at peaceful intervention, armed intervention may be required, preferably by the forces of several nations working together under appropriate regional or international auspices.

We must not allow the legal debate over the technical definition of "genocide" to excuse inaction. The world must act in cases of mass atrocities and mass killing that will eventually lead to genocide even if the local parties are not prepared for peace.

V.   **Prevent Our Enemies from Threatening Us, Our Allies, and Our Friends with Weapons of Mass Destruction**

A. Summary of National Security Strategy 2002

The security environment confronting the United States today is radically different from what we have faced before. Yet the first duty of the United States Government remains what it always has been: to protect the American people and American interests. It is an enduring American principle that this duty obligates the government to anticipate and counter threats, using all elements of national power, before the threats can do grave damage. The greater the threat, the greater is the risk of inaction – and the more compelling the case for taking anticipatory action to defend ourselves, even if uncertainty remains as to the time and place of the enemy's attack. There are few greater threats than a terrorist attack with WMD.

To forestall or prevent such hostile acts by our adversaries, the United States will, if necessary, act preemptively in exercising our inherent right of self-defense. The United States will not resort to force in all cases to preempt emerging threats. Our preference is that nonmilitary actions succeed. And no country should ever use preemption as a pretext for aggression.

Countering proliferation of WMD requires a comprehensive strategy involving strengthened nonproliferation efforts to deny these weapons of terror and related expertise to those seeking them; *proactive counterproliferation efforts* to defend against and defeat WMD and missile threats before they are unleashed; and *improved protection* to mitigate the consequences of WMD use. We aim to convince our adversaries that they cannot achieve their goals with WMD, and thus deter and dissuade them from attempting to use or even acquire these weapons in the first place.

B. Current Context: Successes and Challenges

We have worked hard to protect our citizens and our security. The United States has worked extensively with the international community and key partners to achieve common objectives.

- The United States has begun fielding ballistic missile defenses to deter and protect the United States from missile attacks by rogue states armed with WMD. The fielding of such missile defenses was made possible by the United States' withdrawal from the 1972 Anti-Ballistic Missile Treaty, which was done in accordance with the treaty's provisions.

- In May 2003, the Administration launched the Proliferation Security Initiative (PSI), a global effort that aims to stop shipments of WMD, their delivery systems, and related material. More than 70 countries have expressed support for this initiative, and it has enjoyed several successes in impeding WMD trafficking.

- United States leadership in extensive law enforcement and intelligence cooperation involving several countries led to the roll-up of the A.Q. Khan nuclear network.

- Libya voluntarily agreed to eliminate its WMD programs shortly after a PSI interdiction of a shipment of nuclear-related material from the A.Q. Khan network to Libya.

- The United States led in securing passage in April 2004 of United Nations Security Council (UNSC) Resolution 1540, requiring nations to criminalize WMD proliferation and institute effective export and financial controls.

- We have led the effort to strengthen the ability of the International Atomic Energy Agency (IAEA) to detect and respond to nuclear proliferation.

- The Administration has established a new comprehensive framework, *Biodefense for the 21st Century*, incorporating innovative initiatives to protect the United States against bioterrorism.

Nevertheless, serious challenges remain:

- Iran has violated its Non-Proliferation Treaty safeguards obligations and refuses to provide objective guarantees that its nuclear program is solely for peaceful purposes.

- The DPRK continues to destabilize its region and defy the international community, now boasting a small nuclear arsenal and an illicit nuclear program in violation of its international obligations.

- Terrorists, including those associated with the al-Qaida network, continue to pursue WMD.

- Some of the world's supply of weapons-grade fissile material – the necessary ingredient for making nuclear weapons – is not properly protected.

- Advances in biotechnology provide greater opportunities for state and non-state actors to obtain dangerous pathogens and equipment.

C. The Way Ahead

We are committed to keeping the world's most dangerous weapons out of the hands of the world's most dangerous people.

1. Nuclear Proliferation

The proliferation of nuclear weapons poses the greatest threat to our national security. Nuclear weapons are unique in their capacity to inflict instant loss of life on a massive scale. For this reason, nuclear weapons hold special appeal to rogue states and terrorists.

The best way to block aspiring nuclear states or nuclear terrorists is to deny them access to the essential ingredient of fissile material. It is much harder to deny states or terrorists other key components, for nuclear weapons represent a 60-year old technology and the knowledge is widespread. Therefore, our strategy focuses on controlling fissile material with two priority objectives: first, to keep states from acquiring the capability to produce fissile material suitable for making nuclear weapons; and second, to deter, interdict, or prevent any transfer of that material from states that have this capability to rogue states or to terrorists.

The first objective requires closing a loophole in the Non-Proliferation Treaty that permits regimes to produce fissile material that can be used to make nuclear weapons under cover of a civilian nuclear power program. To close this loophole, we have proposed that the world's leading nuclear exporters create a safe, orderly system that spreads nuclear energy without spreading nuclear weapons. Under this system, all states would have reliable access at reasonable cost to fuel for civilian nuclear power reactors. In return, those states would remain transparent and renounce the enrichment and reprocessing capabilities that can produce fissile material for nuclear weapons. In this way, enrichment and reprocessing will not be necessary for nations seeking to harness nuclear energy for strictly peaceful purposes.

The Administration has worked with the international community in confronting nuclear proliferation.

We may face no greater challenge from a single country than from Iran. For almost 20 years, the Iranian regime hid many of its key nuclear efforts from the international community. Yet the regime continues to claim that it does not seek to develop nuclear weapons. The Iranian regime's true intentions are clearly revealed by the regime's refusal to negotiate in good faith; its refusal to come into compliance with its international obligations by providing the IAEA access to nuclear sites and resolving troubling questions; and the aggressive statements of its President calling for Israel to "be wiped off the face of the earth." The United States has joined with our EU partners and Russia to pressure Iran to meet its international obligations and provide objective guarantees that its nuclear program is only for peaceful purposes. This diplomatic effort must succeed if confrontation is to be avoided.

As important as are these nuclear issues, the United States has broader concerns regarding Iran. The Iranian regime sponsors terrorism; threatens Israel; seeks to thwart Middle East peace; disrupts democracy in Iraq; and denies the aspirations of its people for freedom. The nuclear issue and our other concerns can ultimately be resolved only if the Iranian regime makes the strategic decision to change these policies, open up its political system, and afford freedom to its people. This is the ultimate goal of U.S. policy. In the interim, we will continue to take all necessary measures to protect our national and economic security against the adverse effects of their bad conduct. The problems lie with the illicit behavior and dangerous ambition of the Iranian regime, not the legitimate aspirations and interests of the Iranian people. Our strategy is to block the threats posed by the regime while expanding our engagement and outreach to the people the regime is oppressing.

The North Korean regime also poses a serious nuclear proliferation challenge. It presents a long and bleak record of duplicity and bad-faith negotiations. In the past, the regime has attempted to split the United States from its allies. This time, the United States has successfully forged a consensus among key regional partners – China, Japan, Russia, and the Republic of Korea (ROK) – that the DPRK must give up all of its existing nuclear programs. Regional cooperation offers the best hope for a peaceful, diplomatic resolution of this problem. In a joint statement signed on September 19, 2005, in the Six-Party Talks among these participants, the DPRK agreed to abandon its nuclear weapons and all existing nuclear programs. The joint statement also declared that the relevant parties would negotiate a permanent peace for the Korean peninsula and explore ways to promote security cooperation in Asia. Along with our partners in the Six-Party Talks, the United States will continue to press the DPRK to implement these commitments.

The United States has broader concerns regarding the DPRK as well. The DPRK counterfeits our currency; traffics in narcotics and engages in other illicit activities; threatens the ROK with its army and its neighbors with its missiles; and brutalizes and starves its people. The DPRK regime needs to change these policies, open up its political system, and afford freedom to its people. In the interim, we will continue to take all necessary measures to protect our national and economic security against the adverse effects of their bad conduct.

The second nuclear proliferation objective is to keep fissile material out of the hands of rogue states and terrorists. To do this we must address the danger posed by inadequately safeguarded nuclear and radiological materials worldwide. The Administration is leading a global effort to reduce and secure such materials as quickly as possible through several initiatives including the Global Threat Reduction Initiative (GTRI). The GTRI locates, tracks, and reduces existing stockpiles of nuclear material. This new initiative also discourages trafficking in nuclear material by emplacing detection equipment at key transport nodes.

Building on the success of the PSI, the United States is also leading international efforts to shut down WMD trafficking by targeting key maritime and air transportation and transshipment routes, and by cutting off proliferators from financial resources that support their activities.

2. Biological Weapons

Biological weapons also pose a grave WMD threat because of the risks of contagion that would spread disease across large populations and around the globe. Unlike nuclear weapons, biological weapons do not require hard-to-acquire infrastructure or materials. This makes the challenge of controlling their spread even greater.

Countering the spread of biological weapons requires a strategy focused on improving our capacity to detect and respond to biological attacks, securing dangerous pathogens, and limiting the spread of materials useful for biological weapons. The United States is working with partner nations and institutions to strengthen global biosurveillance capabilities for early detection of suspicious outbreaks of disease. We have launched new initiatives at home to modernize our public health infrastructure and to encourage industry to speed the development of new classes of vaccines and medical countermeasures. This will also enhance our Nation's ability to respond to pandemic public health threats, such as avian influenza.

3. Chemical Weapons

Chemical weapons are a serious proliferation concern and are actively sought by terrorists, including al-Qaida. Much like biological weapons, the threat from chemical weapons increases with advances in technology, improvements in agent development, and ease in acquisition of materials and equipment.

To deter and defend against such threats, we work to identify and disrupt terrorist networks that seek chemical weapons capabilities, and seek to deny them access to materials needed to make these weapons. We are improving our detection and other chemical defense capabilities at home and abroad, including ensuring that U.S. military forces and emergency responders are trained and equipped to manage the consequences of a chemical weapons attack.

4. The Need for Action

The new strategic environment requires new approaches to deterrence and defense. Our deterrence strategy no longer rests primarily on the grim premise of inflicting devastating consequences on potential foes. Both offenses and defenses are necessary to deter state and non-state actors, through denial of the objectives of their attacks and, if necessary, responding with overwhelming force.

Safe, credible, and reliable nuclear forces continue to play a critical role. We are strengthening deterrence by developing a New Triad composed of offensive strike systems (both nuclear and improved conventional capabilities); active and passive defenses, including missile defenses; and a responsive infrastructure, all bound together by enhanced command and control, planning, and intelligence systems. These capabilities will better deter some of the new threats we face, while also bolstering our security commitments to allies. Such security commitments have played a crucial role in convincing some countries to forgo their own nuclear weapons programs, thereby aiding our nonproliferation objectives.

Deterring potential foes and assuring friends and allies, however, is only part of a broader approach. Meeting WMD proliferation challenges also requires effective international action – and the international community is most engaged in such action when the United States leads.

Taking action need not involve military force. Our strong preference and common practice is to address proliferation concerns through international diplomacy, in concert with key allies and regional partners. If necessary, however, under long-standing principles of self defense, we do not rule out the use of force before attacks occur, even if uncertainty remains as to the time and place of the enemy's attack. When the consequences of an attack with WMD are potentially so devastating, we cannot afford to stand idly by as grave dangers materialize. This is the principle and logic of preemption. The place of preemption in our national security strategy remains the same. We will always proceed deliberately, weighing the consequences of our actions. The reasons for our actions will be clear, the force measured, and the cause just.

Iraq and Weapons of Mass Destruction

This Administration inherited an Iraq threat that was unresolved. In early 2001, the international support for U.N. sanctions and continued limits on the Iraqi regime's weapons-related activity was eroding, and key UNSC members were asking that they be lifted.

For America, the September 11 attacks underscored the danger of allowing threats to linger unresolved. Saddam Hussein's continued defiance of 16 UNSC resolutions over 12 years, combined with his record of invading neighboring countries, supporting terrorists, tyrannizing his own people, and using chemical weapons, presented a threat we could no longer ignore.

The UNSC unanimously passed Resolution 1441 on November 8, 2002, calling for full and immediate compliance by the Iraqi regime with its disarmament obligations. Once again, Saddam defied the international community. According to the Iraq Survey Group, the team of inspectors that went into Iraq after Saddam Hussein was toppled and whose report provides the fullest accounting of the Iraqi regime's illicit activities:

"Saddam continued to see the utility of WMD. He explained that he purposely gave an ambiguous impression about possession as a deterrent to Iran. He gave explicit direction to maintain the intellectual capabilities. As U.N. sanctions eroded there was a concomitant expansion of activities that could support full WMD reactivation. He directed that ballistic missile work continue that would support long-range missile development. Virtually no senior Iraqi believed that Saddam had forsaken WMD forever. Evidence suggests that, as resources became available and the constraints of sanctions decayed, there was a direct expansion of activity that would have the effect of supporting future WMD reconstitution."

With the elimination of Saddam's regime, this threat has been addressed, once and for all.

The Iraq Survey Group also found that pre-war intelligence estimates of Iraqi WMD stockpiles were wrong – a conclusion that has been confirmed by a bipartisan commission and congressional investigations. We must learn from this experience if we are to counter successfully the very real threat of proliferation.

First, our intelligence must improve. The President and the Congress have taken steps to reorganize and strengthen the U.S. intelligence community. A single, accountable leader of the intelligence community with authorities to match his responsibilities, and increased sharing of information and increased resources, are helping realize this objective.

Second, there will always be some uncertainty about the status of hidden programs since proliferators are often brutal regimes that go to great lengths to conceal their activities. Indeed, prior to the 1991 Gulf War, many intelligence analysts underestimated the WMD threat posed by the Iraqi regime. After that conflict, they were surprised to learn how far Iraq had progressed along various pathways to try to produce fissile material.

Third, Saddam's strategy of **bluff, denial, and deception is a dangerous game that dictators play at their peril.** The world offered Saddam a clear choice: effect full and immediate compliance with his disarmament obligations or face serious consequences. Saddam chose the latter course and is now facing judgment in an Iraqi court. It was Saddam's reckless behavior that demanded the world's attention, and it was his refusal to remove the ambiguity that he created that forced the United States and its allies to act. We have no doubt that the world is a better place for the removal of this dangerous and unpredictable tyrant, and we have no doubt that the world is better off if tyrants know that they pursue WMD at their own peril.

VI. Ignite a New Era of Global Economic Growth through Free Markets and Free Trade

A. Summary of National Security Strategy 2002

Promoting free and fair trade has long been a bedrock tenet of American foreign policy. Greater economic freedom is ultimately inseparable from political liberty. Economic freedom empowers individuals, and empowered individuals increasingly demand greater political freedom. Greater economic freedom also leads to greater economic opportunity and prosperity for everyone. History has judged the market economy as the single most effective economic system and the greatest antidote to poverty. To expand economic liberty and prosperity, the United States promotes free and fair trade, open markets, a stable financial system, the integration of the global economy, and secure, clean energy development.

B. Current Context: Successes and Challenges

The global economy is more open and free, and many people around the world have seen their lives improve as prosperity and economic integration have increased. The Administration has accomplished much of the economic freedom agenda it set out in 2002:

Seizing the global initiative. We have worked to open markets and integrate the global economy through launching the Doha Development Agenda negotiations of the World Trade Organization (WTO). The United States put forward bold and historic proposals to reform global agricultural trade, to eliminate farm export subsidies and reduce trade-distorting support programs, to eliminate all tariffs on consumer and industrial goods, and to open global services markets. When negotiations stalled in 2003, the United States took the initiative to put Doha back on track, culminating in a successful framework agreement reached in Geneva in 2004. As talks proceed, the United States continues to lead the world in advancing bold proposals for economic freedom through open markets. We also have led the way in helping the accessions of new WTO members such as Armenia, Cambodia, Macedonia, and Saudi Arabia.

Pressing regional and bilateral trade initiatives. We have used FTAs to open markets, support economic reform and the rule of law, and create new opportunities for American farmers and workers. Since 2001, we have:

- Implemented or completed negotiations for FTAs with **14** countries on **5** continents, and are negotiating agreements with **11** additional countries;

- Partnered with Congress to pass the Central America Free Trade Agreement – Dominican Republic (CAFTA-DR), long sought by the leaders of El Salvador, Honduras, Guatemala, Nicaragua, Costa Rica, and Dominican Republic;

- Called in 2003 for the creation of a Middle East Free Trade Area (MEFTA) by 2013 to bring the Middle East into an expanding circle of opportunity;

- Negotiated FTAs with Bahrain, Jordan, Morocco, and Oman to provide a foundation for the MEFTA initiative;

- Launched in 2002 the Enterprise for ASEAN Initiative, which led to the completion of a free trade agreement with Singapore, and the launch of negotiations with Thailand and Malaysia;

- Concluded an FTA with Australia, one of America's strongest allies in the Asia-Pacific region and a major trading partner of the United States; and

- Continued to promote the opportunities of increased trade to sub-Saharan Africa through the African Growth and Opportunity Act (AGOA), and extended opportunity to many other developing countries through the Generalized System of Preferences.

Pressing for open markets, financial stability, and deeper integration of the world economy. We have partnered with Europe, Japan, and other major economies to promote structural reforms that encourage growth, stability, and opportunity across the globe. The United States has:

- Gained agreement in the G-7 on the Agenda for Growth, which commits member states to take concrete steps to reform domestic economic systems;

- Worked with other nations that serve as regional and global engines of growth – such as India, China, the ROK, Brazil, and Russia – on reforms to open markets and ensure financial stability;

- Urged China to move to a market-based, flexible exchange rate regime – a step that would help both China and the global economy; and

- Pressed for reform of the International Financial Institutions to focus on results, fostering good governance and sound policies, and freeing poor countries from unpayable debts.

Enhancing energy security and clean development. The Administration has worked with trading partners and energy producers to expand the types and sources of energy, to open markets and strengthen the rule of law, and to foster private investment that can help develop the energy needed to meet global demand. In addition, we have:

- Worked with industrialized and emerging nations on hydrogen, clean coal, and advanced nuclear technologies; and

- Joined with Australia, China, India, Japan, and the ROK in forming the Asia-Pacific Partnership for Clean Development and Climate to accelerate deployment of clean technologies to enhance energy security, reduce poverty, and reduce pollution.

Several challenges remain:

- Protectionist impulses in many countries put at risk the benefits of open markets and impede the expansion of free and fair trade and economic growth.

- Nations that lack the rule of law are prone to corruption, lack of transparency, and poor governance. These nations frustrate the economic aspirations of their people by failing to promote entrepreneurship, protect intellectual property, or allow their citizens access to vital investment capital.

- Many countries are too dependent upon foreign oil, which is often imported from unstable parts of the world.

- Economic integration spreads wealth across the globe, but also makes local economies more subject to global market conditions.

- Some governments restrict the free flow of capital, subverting the vital role that wise investment can play in promoting economic growth. This denies investments, economic opportunity, and new jobs to the people who need them most.

C. The Way Ahead

Economic freedom is a moral imperative. The liberty to create and build or to buy, sell, and own property is fundamental to human nature and foundational to a free society. Economic freedom also reinforces political freedom. It creates diversified centers of power and authority that limit the reach of government. It expands the free flow of ideas; with increased trade and foreign investment comes exposure to new ways of thinking and living which give citizens more control over their own lives.

To continue extending liberty and prosperity, and to meet the challenges that remain, our strategy going forward involves:

1. Opening markets and integrating developing countries.

While most of the world affirms in principle the appeal of economic liberty, in practice too many nations hold fast to the false comforts of subsidies and trade barriers. Such distortions of the market stifle growth in developed countries, and slow the escape from poverty in developing countries. Against these short-sighted impulses, the United States promotes the enduring vision of a global economy that welcomes all participants and encourages the voluntary exchange of goods and services based on mutual benefit, not favoritism.

We will continue to advance this agenda through the WTO and through bilateral and regional FTAs.

- The United States will seek completion of the Doha Development Agenda negotiations. A successful Doha agreement will expand opportunities for Americans and for others around the world. Trade and open markets will empower citizens in developing countries to improve their lives, while reducing the opportunities for corruption that afflict state-controlled economies.

- We will continue to work with countries such as Russia, Ukraine, Kazakhstan, and Vietnam on the market reforms needed to join the WTO. Participation in the WTO brings opportunities as well as obligations – to strengthen the rule of law and honor the intellectual property rights that sustain the modern knowledge economy, and to remove tariffs, subsidies, and other trade barriers that distort global markets and harm the world's poor.

- We will advance MEFTA by completing and bringing into force FTAs for Bahrain, Oman, and the United Arab Emirates and through other initiatives to expand open trade with and among countries in the region.

- In Africa, we are pursuing an FTA with the countries of the Southern African Customs Union: Botswana, Lesotho, Namibia, South Africa, and Swaziland.

- In Asia, we are pursuing FTAs with Thailand, the ROK, and Malaysia. We will also continue to work closely with China to ensure it honors its WTO commitments and protects intellectual property.

- In our own hemisphere, we will advance the vision of a free trade area of the Americas by building on North American Free Trade Agreement, CAFTA-DR, and the FTA with Chile. We will complete and bring into force FTAs with Colombia, Peru, Ecuador, and Panama.

2. Opening, integrating, and diversifying energy markets to ensure energy independence.

Most of the energy that drives the global economy comes from fossil fuels, especially petroleum. The United States is the world's third largest oil producer, but we rely on international sources to supply more than 50 percent of our needs. Only a small number of countries make major contributions to the world's oil supply.

The world's dependence on these few suppliers is neither responsible nor sustainable over the long term. The key to ensuring our energy security is *diversity* in the regions from which energy resources come and in the types of energy resources on which we rely.

- The Administration will work with resource-rich countries to increase their openness, transparency, and rule of law. This will promote effective democratic governance and attract the investment essential to developing their resources and expanding the range of energy suppliers.

- We will build the Global Nuclear Energy Partnership to work with other nations to develop and deploy advanced nuclear recycling and reactor technologies. This initiative will help provide reliable, emission-free energy with less of the waste burden of older technologies and without making available separated plutonium that could be used by rogue states or terrorists for nuclear weapons. These new technologies will make possible a dramatic expansion of safe, clean nuclear energy to help meet the growing global energy demand.

- We will work with international partners to develop other transformational technologies such as clean coal and hydrogen. Through projects like our FutureGen initiative, we seek to turn our abundant domestic coal into emissions-free sources of electricity and hydrogen, providing our economies increased power with decreased emissions.

- On the domestic front, we are investing in zero-emission coal-fired plants; revolutionary solar and wind technologies; clean, safe nuclear energy; and cutting-edge methods of producing ethanol.

Our comprehensive energy strategy puts a priority on reducing our reliance on foreign energy sources. Diversification of energy sources also will help alleviate the "petroleum curse" – the tendency for oil revenues to foster corruption and prevent economic growth and political reform in some oil-producing states. In too many such nations, ruling elites enrich themselves while denying the people the benefits of their countries' natural wealth. In the worst cases, oil revenues fund activities that destabilize their regions or advance violent ideologies. Diversifying the suppliers within and across regions reduces opportunities for corruption and diminishes the leverage of irresponsible rulers.

3. Reforming the International Financial System to Ensure Stability and Growth

In our interconnected world, stable and open financial markets are an essential feature of a prosperous global economy. We will work to improve the stability and openness of markets by:

- **Promoting Growth-Oriented Economic Policies Worldwide**. Sound policies in the United States have helped drive much international growth. We cannot be the only source of strength, however. We will work with the world's other major economies, including the EU and Japan, to promote structural reforms that open their markets and increase productivity in their nations and across the world.

- **Encouraging Adoption of Flexible Exchange Rates and Open Markets for Financial Services**. The United States will help emerging economies make the transition to the flexible exchange rates appropriate for major economies. In particular, we will continue to urge China to meet its own commitment to a market-based, flexible exchange rate regime. We will also promote more open financial service markets, which encourage stable and sound financial practices.

- **Strengthening International Financial Institutions**. At the dawn of a previous era 6 decades ago, the United States championed the creation of the World Bank and the International Monetary Fund (IMF). These institutions were instrumental in the development of the global economy and an expansion of prosperity unprecedented in world history. They remain vital today, but must adapt to new realities:

  - For the World Bank and regional development banks, we will encourage greater emphasis on investments in the private sector. We will urge more consideration of economic freedom, governance, and measurable results in allocating funds. We will promote an increased use of grants to relieve the burden of unsustainable debt.

  - For the IMF, we will seek to refocus it on its core mission: international financial stability. This means strengthening the IMF's ability to monitor the financial system to prevent crises before they happen. If crises occur, the IMF's response must reinforce each country's responsibility for its own economic choices. A refocused IMF will strengthen market institutions and market discipline over financial decisions, helping to promote a stable and prosperous global economy. By doing so, over time markets and the private sector can supplant the need for the IMF to perform in its current role.

- **Building Local Capital Markets and the Formal Economy in the Developing World**. The first place that small businesses in developing countries turn to for resources is their own domestic markets. Unfortunately, in too many countries these resources are unavailable due to weak financial systems, a lack of property rights, and the diversion of economic activity away from the formal economy into the black market. The United States will work with these countries to develop and strengthen local capital markets and reduce the black market. This will provide more resources to helping the public sector govern effectively and the private sector grow and prosper.

- **Creating a More Transparent, Accountable, and Secure International Financial System**. The United States has worked with public and private partners to help secure the international financial system against abuse by criminals, terrorists, money launderers, and corrupt political leaders. We will continue to use international venues like the Financial Action Task Force to ensure that this global system is transparent and protected from abuse by tainted capital. We must also develop new tools that allow us to detect, disrupt, and isolate rogue financial players and gatekeepers.

VII. **Expand the Circle of Development by Opening Societies and Building the Infrastructure of Democracy**

A. Summary of National Security Strategy 2002

Helping the world's poor is a strategic priority and a moral imperative. Economic development, responsible governance, and individual liberty are intimately connected. Past foreign assistance to corrupt and ineffective governments failed to help the populations in greatest need. Instead, it often impeded democratic reform and encouraged corruption. The United States must promote development programs that achieve measurable results – rewarding reforms, encouraging transparency, and improving people's lives. Led by the United States, the international community has endorsed this approach in the Monterrey Consensus.

B. Current Context: Successes and Challenges

The United States has improved the lives of millions of people and transformed the practice of development by adopting more effective policies and programs.

- **Advancing Development and Reinforcing Reform.** The Administration pioneered a revolution in development strategy with the Millennium Challenge Account program, rewarding countries that govern justly, invest in their people, and foster economic freedom. The program is based on the principle that each nation bears the responsibility for its own development. It offers governments the opportunity and the means to undertake transformational change by designing their own reform and development programs, which are then funded through the Millennium Challenge Corporation (MCC). The MCC has approved over $1.5 billion for compacts in eight countries, is working with over a dozen other countries on compacts, and has committed many smaller grants to other partner countries.

- **Turning the Tide Against AIDS and Other Infectious Diseases.** The President's Emergency Plan for AIDS Relief is an unprecedented, 5-year, $15 billion effort. Building on the success of pioneering programs in Africa, we have launched a major initiative that will prevent 7 million new infections, provide treatment to 2 million infected individuals, and care for 10 million AIDS orphans and others affected by the disease. We have launched a $1.2 billion, 5-year initiative to reduce malaria deaths by 50 percent in at least 15 targeted countries. To mobilize other nations and the private sector, the United States pioneered the creation of the Global Fund to Fight HIV/AIDS, Tuberculosis, and Malaria. We are the largest donor to the Fund and have already contributed over $1.4 billion.

- **Promoting Debt Sustainability and a Path Toward Private Capital Markets.** The Administration has sought to break the burden of debt that traps many poor countries by encouraging international financial institutions to provide grants instead of loans to low-income nations. With the United Kingdom, we spearheaded the G-8 initiative to provide 100 percent multilateral debt relief to qualifying Heavily Indebted Poor

Countries. Reducing debt to sustainable levels allows countries to focus on immediate development challenges. In the long run, reducing debt also opens access to private capital markets which foster sound policies and long-term growth.

- **Addressing Urgent Needs and Investing in People.** The United States leads the world in providing food relief. We launched the Initiative to End Hunger in Africa, using science, technology, and market incentives to increase the productivity of African farmers. We launched a 3-year, $900 million initiative to provide clean water to the poor. We have tripled basic education assistance through programs such as the Africa Education Initiative, which will train teachers and administrators, build schools, buy textbooks, and expand opportunities inside and outside the classroom.

- **Unleashing the Power of the Private Sector.** The Administration has sought to multiply the impact of our development assistance through initiatives such as the Global Development Alliance, which forges partnerships with the private sector to advance development goals, and Volunteers for Prosperity, which enlists some of our Nation's most capable professionals to serve strategically in developing nations.

- **Fighting Corruption and Promoting Transparency.** Through multilateral efforts like the G-8 Transparency Initiative and our policy of denying corrupt foreign officials entry into the United States, we are helping ensure that organized crime and parasitic rulers do not choke off the benefits of economic assistance and growth.

We have increased our overall development assistance spending by 97 percent since 2000. In all of these efforts, the United States has sought concrete measures of success. Funding is a means, not the end. We are giving more money to help the world's poor, and giving it more effectively.

Many challenges remain, including:

- Helping millions of people in the world who continue to suffer from poverty and disease;

- Ensuring that the delivery of assistance reinforces good governance and sound economic policies; and

- Building the capacity of poor countries to take ownership of their own development strategies.

C. The Way Ahead

America's national interests and moral values drive us in the same direction: to assist the world's poor citizens and least developed nations and help integrate them into the global economy. We have accomplished many of the goals laid out in the 2002 National Security Strategy. Many of the new initiatives we launched in the last 4 years are now fully operating to help the plight of the world's least fortunate. We will persevere on this path.

Development reinforces diplomacy and defense, reducing long-term threats to our national security by helping to build stable, prosperous, and peaceful societies. Improving the way we use foreign assistance will make it more effective in strengthening responsible governments, responding to suffering, and improving people's lives.

1. Transformational Diplomacy and Effective Democracy

Transformational diplomacy means working with our many international partners to build and sustain democratic, well-governed states that will respond to the needs of their citizens and conduct themselves responsibly in the international system. Long-term development must include encouraging governments to make wise choices and assisting them in implementing those choices. We will encourage and reward good behavior rather than reinforce negative behavior. Ultimately it is the countries themselves that must decide to take the necessary steps toward development, yet we will help advance this process by creating external incentives for governments to reform themselves.

Effective economic development advances our national security by helping promote responsible sovereignty, not permanent dependency. Weak and impoverished states and ungoverned areas are not only a threat to their people and a burden on regional economies, but are also susceptible to exploitation by terrorists, tyrants, and international criminals. We will work to bolster threatened states, provide relief in times of crisis, and build capacity in developing states to increase their progress.

2. Making Foreign Assistance More Effective

The Administration has created the new position of Director of Foreign Assistance (DFA) in the State Department. The DFA will serve concurrently as Administrator of U.S. Agency for International Development (USAID), a position that will continue to be at the level of Deputy Secretary, and will have, consistent with existing legal requirements, authority over all State Department and USAID foreign assistance. This reorganization will create a more unified and rational structure that will more fully align assistance programs in State and USAID, increase the effectiveness of these programs for recipient countries, and ensure that we are being the best possible stewards of taxpayer dollars. And it will focus our foreign assistance on promoting greater ownership and responsibility on the part of host nations and their citizens.

With this new authority, the DFA/Administrator will develop a coordinated foreign assistance strategy, including 5-year, country-specific assistance strategies and annual country-specific assistance operational plans. The DFA/Administrator also will provide guidance for the assistance delivered through other entities of the United States Government, including the MCC and the Office of the Global AIDS Coordinator.

To ensure the best stewardship of our foreign assistance, the United States will:

- Distinguish among the different challenges facing different nations and address those challenges with tools appropriate for each country's stage of development;

- Encourage and reward good government and economic reform, both bilaterally and through the multilateral institutions such as international financial institutions, the G-8, and the Asia-Pacific Economic Cooperation (APEC);

- Engage the private sector to help solve development problems;

- Promote graduation from economic aid dependency with the ultimate goal of ending assistance;

- Build trade capacity to enable the poorest countries to enter into the global trade system; and

- Empower local leaders to take responsibility for their country's development.

Our assistance efforts will also highlight and build on the lessons learned from successful examples of wise development and economic policy choices, such as the ROK, Taiwan, Ireland, Poland, Slovakia, Chile, and Botswana.

VIII. Develop Agendas for Cooperative Action with the Other Main Centers of Global Power

A. Summary of National Security Strategy 2002

Relations with the most powerful countries in the world are central to our national security strategy. Our priority is pursuing American interests within cooperative relationships, particularly with our oldest and closest friends and allies. At the same time, we must seize the opportunity – unusual in historical terms – of an absence of fundamental conflict between the great powers. Another priority, therefore, is preventing the reemergence of the great power rivalries that divided the world in previous eras. New times demand new approaches, flexible enough to permit effective action even when there are reasonable differences of opinions among friends, yet strong enough to confront the challenges the world faces.

B. Current Context: Successes and Challenges

The United States has enjoyed unprecedented levels of cooperation on many of its highest national security priorities:

- The global coalition against terror has grown and deepened, with extensive cooperation and common resolve. The nations that have partnered with us in Afghanistan and Iraq have developed capabilities that can be applied to other challenges.

- We have joined with other nations around the world as well as numerous multilateral organizations to improve the capability of all nations to defend their homelands against terrorists and transnational criminals.

- We have achieved extraordinary coordination among historic rivals in pressing the DPRK to abandon its nuclear program.

- We have partnered with European allies and international institutions to pressure Iran to honor its non-proliferation commitments.

- The North Atlantic Treaty Organization (NATO) is transforming itself to meet current threats and is playing a leading role in stabilizing the Balkans and Afghanistan, as well as training the Iraqi military leadership to address its security challenges.

- We have set aside decades of mistrust and put relations with India, the world's most populous democracy, on a new and fruitful path.

At the same time, America's relations with other nations have been strong enough to withstand differences and candid exchanges of views.

- Some of our oldest and closest friends disagreed with U.S. policy in Iraq. There are ongoing and serious debates with our allies about how best to address the unique and evolving nature of the global terrorist threat.

- We have disagreed on the steps to reduce agricultural subsidies and achieve success in the WTO Doha Round of trade negotiations. We have also faced challenges in forging consensus with other major nations on the most effective measures to protect the environment.

C. The Way Ahead

The struggle against militant Islamic radicalism is the great ideological conflict of the early years of the 21st century and finds the great powers all on the same side – opposing the terrorists. This circumstance differs profoundly from the ideological struggles of the 20th century, which saw the great powers divided by ideology as well as by national interest.

The potential for great power consensus presents the United States with an extraordinary opportunity. Yet certain challenges must be overcome. Some nations differ with us on the appropriate pace of change. Other nations provide rhetorical support for free markets and effective democracy but little action on freedom's behalf.

Five principles undergird our strategy for relations with the main centers of global power.

- First, these relations must be set in their proper context. Bilateral policies that ignore regional and global realities are unlikely to succeed.

- Second, these relations must be supported by appropriate institutions, regional and global, to make cooperation more permanent, effective, and wide-reaching. Where existing institutions can be reformed to meet new challenges, we, along with our partners, must reform them. Where appropriate institutions do not exist, we, along with our partners, must create them.

- Third, we cannot pretend that our interests are unaffected by states' treatment of their own citizens. America's interest in promoting effective democracies rests on an historical fact: states that are governed well are most inclined to behave well. We will encourage all our partners to expand liberty, and to respect the rule of law and the dignity of the individual, as the surest way to advance the welfare of their people and to cement close relations with the United States.

- Fourth, while we do not seek to dictate to other states the choices they make, we do seek to influence the calculations on which these choices are based. We also must hedge appropriately in case states choose unwisely.

- Fifth, we must be prepared to act alone if necessary, while recognizing that there is little of lasting consequence that we can accomplish in the world without the sustained cooperation of our allies and partners.

1. The Western Hemisphere

These principles guide our relations within our own Hemisphere, the frontline of defense of American national security. Our goal remains a hemisphere fully democratic, bound together by good will, security cooperation, and the opportunity for all our citizens to prosper. Tyrants and those who would follow them belong to a different era and must not be allowed to reverse the progress of the last two decades. Countries in the Hemisphere must be helped to the path of sustained political and economic development. The deceptive appeal of anti-free market populism must not be allowed to erode political freedoms and trap the Hemisphere's poorest in cycles of poverty. If America's nearest neighbors are not secure and stable, then Americans will be less secure.

Our strategy for the Hemisphere begins with deepening key relationships with Canada and Mexico, a foundation of shared values and cooperative policies that can be extended throughout the region. We must continue to work with our neighbors in the Hemisphere to reduce illegal immigration and promote expanded economic opportunity for marginalized populations. We must also solidify strategic relationships with regional leaders in Central and South America and the Caribbean who are deepening their commitment to democratic values. And we must continue to work with regional partners to make multilateral institutions like the OAS and the Inter-American Development Bank more effective and better able to foster concerted action to address threats that may arise to the region's stability, security, prosperity, or democratic progress. Together, these partnerships can advance our four strategic priorities for the region: bolstering security, strengthening democratic institutions, promoting prosperity, and investing in people.

2. Africa

Africa holds growing geo-strategic importance and is a high priority of this Administration. It is a place of promise and opportunity, linked to the United States by history, culture, commerce, and strategic significance. Our goal is an African continent that knows liberty, peace, stability, and increasing prosperity.

Africa's potential has in the past been held hostage by the bitter legacy of colonial misrule and bad choices by some African leaders. The United States recognizes that our security depends upon partnering with Africans to strengthen fragile and failing states and bring ungoverned areas under the control of effective democracies.

Overcoming the challenges Africa faces requires partnership, not paternalism. Our strategy is to promote economic development and the expansion of effective, democratic governance so that African states can take the lead in addressing African challenges. Through improved governance, reduced corruption, and market reforms, African nations can lift themselves toward a better future. We are committed to working with African nations to strengthen their domestic capabilities and the regional capacity of the AU to support post-conflict transformations, consolidate democratic transitions, and improve peacekeeping and disaster responses.

3. Middle East

The Broader Middle East continues to command the world's attention. For too long, too many nations of the Middle East have suffered from a freedom deficit. Repression has fostered corruption, imbalanced or stagnant economies, political resentments, regional conflicts, and religious extremism. These maladies were all cloaked by an illusion of stability. Yet the peoples of the Middle East share the same desires as people in the rest of the world: liberty, opportunity, justice, order, and peace. These desires are now being expressed in movements for reform. The United States is committed to supporting the efforts of reformers to realize a better life for themselves and their region.

We seek a Middle East of independent states, at peace with each other, and fully participating in an open global market of goods, services, and ideas. We are seeking to build a framework that will allow Israel and the Palestinian territories to live side by side in peace and security as two democratic states. In the wider region, we will continue to support efforts for reform and freedom in traditional allies such as Egypt and Saudi Arabia. Tyrannical regimes such as Iran and Syria that oppress at home and sponsor terrorism abroad know that we will continue to stand with their people against their misrule. And in Iraq, we will continue to support the Iraqi people and their historic march from tyranny to effective democracy. We will work with the freely elected, democratic government of Iraq – our new partner in the War on Terror – to consolidate and expand freedom, and to build security and lasting stability.

4. Europe

The North Atlantic Treaty Organization remains a vital pillar of U.S. foreign policy. The Alliance has been strengthened by expanding its membership and now acts beyond its borders as an instrument for peace and stability in many parts of the world. It has also established partnerships with other key European states, including Russia, Ukraine, and others, further extending NATO's historic transformation. The internal reform of NATO structures, capabilities, and procedures must be accelerated to ensure that NATO is able to carry out its missions effectively. The Alliance's door will also remain open to those countries that aspire for membership and meet NATO standards. Further, NATO must deepen working relationships between and across institutions, as it is doing with the EU, and as it also could do with new institutions. Such relationships offer opportunities for enhancing the distinctive strengths and missions of each organization.

Europe is home to some of our oldest and closest allies. Our cooperative relations are built on a sure foundation of shared values and interests. This foundation is expanding and deepening with the ongoing spread of effective democracies in Europe, and must expand and deepen still further if we are to reach the goal of a Europe whole, free, and at peace. These democracies are effective partners, joining with us to promote global freedom and prosperity. Just as in the special relationship that binds us to the United Kingdom, these cooperative relationships forge deeper ties between our nations.

5. Russia

The United States seeks to work closely with Russia on strategic issues of common interest and to manage issues on which we have differing interests. By reason of geography and power, Russia has great influence not only in Europe and its own immediate neighborhood, but also in many other regions of vital interest to us: the broader Middle East, South and Central Asia, and East Asia. We must encourage Russia to respect the values of freedom and democracy at home and not to impede the cause of freedom and democracy in these regions. Strengthening our relationship will depend on the policies, foreign and domestic, that Russia adopts. Recent trends regrettably point toward a diminishing commitment to democratic freedoms and institutions. We will work to try to persuade the Russian Government to move forward, not backward, along freedom's path.

Stability and prosperity in Russia's neighborhood will help deepen our relations with Russia; but that stability will remain elusive as long as this region is not governed by effective democracies. We will seek to persuade Russia's government that democratic progress in Russia and its region benefits the peoples who live there and improves relationships with us, with other Western governments, and among themselves. Conversely, efforts to prevent democratic development at home and abroad will hamper the development of Russia's relations with the United States, Europe, and its neighbors.

6. South and Central Asia

South and Central Asia is a region of great strategic importance where American interests and values are engaged as never before. India is a great democracy, and our shared values are the foundation of our good relations. We are eager to see Pakistan move along a stable, secure, and democratic path. Our goal is for the entire region of South and Central Asia to be democratic, prosperous, and at peace.

We have made great strides in transforming America's relationship with India, a major power that shares our commitment to freedom, democracy, and rule of law. In July 2005, we signed a bold agreement – a roadmap to realize the meaningful cooperation that had eluded our two nations for decades. India now is poised to shoulder global obligations in cooperation with the United States in a way befitting a major power.

Progress with India has been achieved even as the United States has improved its strategic relationship with Pakistan. For decades, outsiders acted as if good relations with India and Pakistan were mutually exclusive. This Administration has shown that improved relations with each are possible and can help India and Pakistan make strides toward a lasting peace between themselves. America's relationship with Pakistan will not be a mirror image of our relationship with India. Together, our relations with the nations of South Asia can serve as a foundation for deeper engagement throughout

Central Asia. Increasingly, Afghanistan will assume its historical role as a land-bridge between South and Central Asia, connecting these two vital regions.

Central Asia is an enduring priority for our foreign policy. The five countries of Central Asia are distinct from one another and our relations with each, while important, will differ. In the region as a whole, the elements of our larger strategy meet, and we must pursue those elements simultaneously: promoting effective democracies and the expansion of free-market reforms, diversifying global sources of energy, and enhancing security and winning the War on Terror.

7. East Asia

East Asia is a region of great opportunities and lingering tensions. Over the past decade, it has been a source of extraordinary economic dynamism and also of economic turbulence. Few regional economies have more effectively harnessed the engines of future prosperity: technology and globalized trade. Yet few regions have had greater difficulty overcoming the suspicions of the past.

The United States is a Pacific nation, with extensive interests throughout East and Southeast Asia. The region's stability and prosperity depend on our sustained engagement: maintaining robust partnerships supported by a forward defense posture supporting economic integration through expanded trade and investment and promoting democracy and human rights.

Forging new international initiatives and institutions can assist in the spread of freedom, prosperity, and regional security. Existing institutions like the APEC forum and the Association of Southeast Asian Nations (ASEAN) Regional Forum, can play a vital role. New arrangements, such as the U.S.-ASEAN Enhanced Partnership, or others that are focused on problem-solving and action, like the Six-Party Talks and the PSI, can likewise bring together Asian nations to address common challenges. And Asian nations that share our values can join us in partnership to strengthen new democracies and promote democratic reforms throughout the region. This institutional framework, however, must be built upon a foundation of sound bilateral relations with key states in the region.

With Japan, the United States enjoys the closest relations in a generation. As the world's two largest economies and aid donors, acting in concert multiplies each of our strengths and magnifies our combined contributions to global progress. Our shared commitment to democracy at home offers a sure foundation for cooperation abroad.

With Australia, our alliance is global in scope. From Iraq and Afghanistan to our historic FTA, we are working jointly to ensure security, prosperity, and expanded liberty.

With the ROK, we share a vision of a prosperous, democratic, and united Korean peninsula. We also share a commitment to democracy at home and progress abroad and are translating that common vision into joint action to sustain our alliance into the 21st century.

With Southeast Asia, we celebrate the dynamism of increased economic freedom and look to further extend political freedom to all the people in the region, including those suffering under the repressive regime in Burma. In promoting greater economic and political liberty, we will work closely with our allies and key friends, including Indonesia, Malaysia, the Philippines, Singapore, and Thailand.

China encapsulates Asia's dramatic economic successes, but China's transition remains incomplete. In one generation, China has gone from poverty and isolation to growing integration into the international economic system. China once opposed global institutions; today it is a permanent member of the UNSC and the WTO. As China becomes a global player, it must act as a responsible stakeholder that fulfills its obligations and works with the United States and others to advance the international system that has enabled its success: enforcing the international rules that have helped China lift itself out of a century of economic deprivation, embracing the economic and political standards that go along with that system of rules, and contributing to international stability and security by working with the United States and other major powers.

China's leaders proclaim that they have made a decision to walk the transformative path of peaceful development. If China keeps this commitment, the United States will welcome the emergence of a China that is peaceful and prosperous and that cooperates with us to address common challenges and mutual interests. China can make an important contribution to global prosperity and ensure its own prosperity for the longer term if it will rely more on domestic demand and less on global trade imbalances to drive its economic growth. China shares our exposure to the challenges of globalization and other transnational concerns. Mutual interests can guide our cooperation on issues such as terrorism, proliferation, and energy security. We will work to increase our cooperation to combat disease pandemics and reverse environmental degradation.

The United States encourages China to continue down the road of reform and openness, because in this way China's leaders can meet the legitimate needs and aspirations of the Chinese people for liberty, stability, and prosperity. As economic growth continues, China will face a growing demand from its own people to follow the path of East Asia's many modern democracies, adding political freedom to economic freedom. Continuing along this path will contribute to regional and international security.

China's leaders must realize, however, that they cannot stay on this peaceful path while holding on to old ways of thinking and acting that exacerbate concerns throughout the region and the world. These old ways include:

- Continuing China's military expansion in a non-transparent way;

- Expanding trade, but acting as if they can somehow "lock up" energy supplies around the world or seek to direct markets rather than opening them up – as if they can follow a mercantilism borrowed from a discredited era; and

- Supporting resource-rich countries without regard to the misrule at home or misbehavior abroad of those regimes.

China and Taiwan must also resolve their differences peacefully, without coercion and without unilateral action by either China or Taiwan.

Ultimately, China's leaders must see that they cannot let their population increasingly experience the freedoms to buy, sell, and produce, while denying them the rights to assemble, speak, and worship. Only by allowing the Chinese people to enjoy these basic freedoms and universal rights can China honor its own constitution and international commitments and reach its full potential. Our strategy seeks to encourage China to make the right strategic choices for its people, while we hedge against other possibilities.

IX. **Transform America's National Security Institutions to Meet the Challenges and Opportunities of the 21st Century**

A. Summary of National Security Strategy 2002

The major institutions of American national security were designed in a different era to meet different challenges. They must be transformed.

B. Current Context: Successes and Challenges

In the last four years, we have made substantial progress in transforming key national security institutions.

- The establishment of the Department of Homeland Security brought under one authority 22 federal entities with vital roles to play in protecting our Nation and preventing terrorist attacks within the United States. The Department is focused on three national security priorities: preventing terrorist attacks within the United States; reducing America's vulnerability to terrorism; and minimizing the damage and facilitating the recovery from attacks that do occur.

- In 2004, the Intelligence Community launched its most significant reorganization since the 1947 National Security Act. The centerpiece is a new position, the Director of National Intelligence, endowed with expanded budgetary, acquisition, tasking, and personnel authorities to integrate more effectively the efforts of the Community into a more unified, coordinated, and effective whole. The transformation also includes a new National Counterterrorism Center and a new National Counterproliferation Center to manage and coordinate planning and activities in those critical areas. The transformation extends to the FBI, which has augmented its intelligence capabilities and is now more fully and effectively integrated with the Intelligence Community.

- The Department of Defense has completed the 2006 Quadrennial Defense Review, which details how the Department will continue to adapt and build to meet new challenges.

  - We are pursuing a future force that will provide tailored deterrence of both state and non-state threats (including WMD employment, terrorist attacks in the physical and information domains, and opportunistic aggression) while assuring allies and dissuading potential competitors. The Department of Defense also is expanding Special Operations Forces and investing in advanced conventional capabilities to help win the long war against terrorist extremists and to help dissuade any hostile military competitor from challenging the United States, its allies, and partners.

  - The Department is transforming itself to better balance its capabilities across four categories of challenges:

- **Traditional** challenges posed by states employing conventional armies, navies, and air forces in well-established forms of military competition.

- **Irregular** challenges from state and non-state actors employing methods such as terrorism and insurgency to counter our traditional military advantages, or engaging in criminal activity such as piracy and drug trafficking that threaten regional security.

- **Catastrophic** challenges involving the acquisition, possession, and use of WMD by state and non-state actors; and deadly pandemics and other natural disasters that produce WMD-like effects.

- **Disruptive** challenges from state and non-state actors who employ technologies and capabilities (such as biotechnology, cyber and space operations, or directed-energy weapons) in new ways to counter military advantages the United States currently enjoys.

C. The Way Ahead

We must extend and enhance the transformation of key institutions, both domestically and abroad.

At home, we will pursue three priorities:

- ***Sustaining the transformation already under way in the Departments of Defense, Homeland Security, and Justice; the Federal Bureau of Investigation; and the Intelligence Community.***

- ***Continuing to reorient the Department of State towards transformational diplomacy,*** which promotes effective democracy and responsible sovereignty. Our diplomats must be able to step outside their traditional role to become more involved with the challenges within other societies, helping them directly, channeling assistance, and learning from their experience. This effort will include:

  - Promoting the efforts of the new Director for Foreign Assistance/Administrator to ensure that foreign assistance is used as effectively as possible to meet our broad foreign policy objectives. This new office will align more fully the foreign assistance activities carried out by the Department of State and USAID, demonstrating that we are responsible stewards of taxpayer dollars.

  - Improving our capability to plan for and respond to post-conflict and failed-state situations. The Office of Reconstruction and Stabilization will integrate all relevant United States Government resources and assets in conducting reconstruction and stabilization operations. This effort must focus on building the security and law enforcement structures that are often the prerequisite for restoring order and ensuring success.

- Developing a civilian reserve corps, analogous to the military reserves. The civilian reserve corps would utilize, in a flexible and timely manner, the human resources of the American people for skills and capacities needed for international disaster relief and post-conflict reconstruction.

- Strengthening our public diplomacy, so that we advocate the policies and values of the United States in a clear, accurate, and persuasive way to a watching and listening world. This includes actively engaging foreign audiences, expanding educational opportunities for Americans to learn about foreign languages and cultures and for foreign students and scholars to study in the United States; empowering the voices of our citizen ambassadors as well as those foreigners who share our commitment to a safer, more compassionate world; enlisting the support of the private sector; increasing our channels for dialogue with Muslim leaders and citizens; and confronting propaganda quickly, before myths and distortions have time to take root in the hearts and minds of people across the world.

- *Improving the capacity of agencies to plan, prepare, coordinate, integrate, and execute responses* covering the full range of crisis contingencies and long-term challenges.

  - We need to strengthen the capacity of departments and agencies to do comprehensive, results-oriented planning.

  - Agencies that traditionally played only a domestic role increasingly have a role to play in our foreign and security policies. This requires us to better integrate interagency activity both at home and abroad.

Abroad, we will work with our allies on three priorities:

- *Promoting meaningful reform of the U.N.*, including:

  - Creating structures to ensure financial accountability and administrative and organizational efficiency.

  - Enshrining the principle that membership and participation privileges are earned by responsible behavior and by reasonable burden-sharing of security and stability challenges.

  - Enhancing the capacity of the U.N. and associated regional organizations to stand up well-trained, rapidly deployable, sustainable military and gendarme units for peace operations.

- Ensuring that the U.N. reflects today's geopolitical realities and is not shackled by obsolete structures.

- Reinvigorating the U.N.'s commitment, reflected in the U.N. Charter, to the promotion of democracy and human rights.

- ***Enhancing the role of democracies and democracy promotion throughout international and multilateral institutions***, including:

  - Strengthening and institutionalizing the Community of Democracies.

  - Fostering the creation of regional democracy-based institutions in Asia, the Middle East, Africa, and elsewhere.

  - Improving the capacity of the U.N. and other multilateral institutions to advance the freedom agenda through tools like the U.N. Democracy Fund.

  - Coordinating more effectively the unique contributions of international financial institutions and regional development banks.

- ***Establishing results-oriented partnerships*** on the model of the PSI ***to meet new challenges and opportunities***. These partnerships emphasize international cooperation, not international bureaucracy. They rely on voluntary adherence rather than binding treaties. They are oriented towards action and results rather than legislation or rule-making.

X. **Engage the Opportunities and Confront the Challenges of Globalization**

In recent years, the world has witnessed the growing importance of a set of opportunities and challenges that were addressed indirectly in National Security Strategy 2002: the national security implications of globalization.

Globalization presents many opportunities. Much of the world's prosperity and improved living standards in recent years derive from the expansion of global trade, investment, information, and technology. The United States has been a leader in promoting these developments, and we believe they have improved significantly the quality of life of the American people and people the world over. Other nations have embraced these opportunities and have likewise benefited. Globalization has also helped the advance of democracy by extending the marketplace of ideas and the ideals of liberty.

These new flows of trade, investment, information, and technology are transforming national security. Globalization has exposed us to new challenges and changed the way old challenges touch our interests and values, while also greatly enhancing our capacity to respond. Examples include:

- *Public health challenges like pandemics (HIV/AIDS, avian influenza) that recognize no borders*. The risks to social order are so great that traditional public health approaches may be inadequate, necessitating new strategies and responses.

- *Illicit trade, whether in drugs, human beings, or sex, that exploits the modern era's greater ease of transport and exchange.* Such traffic corrodes social order; bolsters crime and corruption; undermines effective governance; facilitates the illicit transfer of WMD and advanced conventional weapons technology; and compromises traditional security and law enforcement.

- *Environmental destruction, whether caused by human behavior or cataclysmic mega-disasters such as floods, hurricanes, earthquakes, or tsunamis.* Problems of this scope may overwhelm the capacity of local authorities to respond, and may even overtax national militaries, requiring a larger international response.

These challenges are not traditional national security concerns, such as the conflict of arms or ideologies. But if left unaddressed they can threaten national security. We have learned that:

- Preparing for and managing these challenges requires the full exercise of national power, up to and including traditional security instruments. For example, the U.S. military provided critical logistical support in the response to the Southeast Asian tsunami and the South Asian earthquake until U.N. and civilian humanitarian responders could relieve the military of these vital duties.

- Technology can help, but the key to rapid and effective response lies in achieving unity of effort across a range of agencies. For example, our response to the Katrina and Rita hurricanes underscored the need for communications systems that remain operational and integrated during times of crisis. Even more vital, however, is improved coordination within the Federal government, with state and local partners, and with the private sector.

- Existing international institutions have a role to play, but in many cases coalitions of the willing may be able to respond more quickly and creatively, at least in the short term. For example, U.S. leadership in mobilizing the Regional Core Group to respond to the tsunami of 2004 galvanized the follow-on international response.

- The response and the new partnerships it creates can sometimes serve as a catalyst for changing existing political conditions to address other problems. For example, the response to the tsunami in Southeast Asia and the earthquake in Pakistan developed new lines of communication and cooperation at a local level, which opened the door to progress in reconciling long-standing regional conflicts in Aceh and the Kashmir.

Effective democracies are better able to deal with these challenges than are repressive or poorly governed states. Pandemics require robust and fully transparent public health systems, which weak governments and those that fear freedom are unable or unwilling to provide. Yet these challenges require effective democracies to come together in innovative ways.

The United States must lead the effort to reform existing institutions and create new ones – including forging new partnerships between governmental and nongovernmental actors, and with transnational and international organizations.

To confront illicit trade, for example, the Administration launched the Proliferation Security Initiative and the APEC Secure Trade in the APEC Region Initiative, both of which focus on tangible steps governments can take to combat illegal trade.

To combat the cultivation and trafficking of narcotics, the Administration devotes over $1 billion annually to comprehensive counternarcotics efforts, working with governments, particularly in Latin America and Asia, to eradicate crops, destroy production facilities, interdict shipments, and support developing alternative livelihoods.

To confront the threat of a possible pandemic, the Administration took the lead in creating the International Partnership on Avian and Pandemic Influenza, a new global partnership of states committed to effective surveillance and preparedness that will help to detect and respond quickly to any outbreaks of the disease.

XI. Conclusion

The challenges America faces are great, yet we have enormous power and influence to address those challenges. The times require an ambitious national security strategy, yet one recognizing the limits to what even a nation as powerful as the United States can achieve by itself. Our national security strategy is idealistic about goals, and realistic about means.

There was a time when two oceans seemed to provide protection from problems in other lands, leaving America to lead by example alone. That time has long since passed. America cannot know peace, security, and prosperity by retreating from the world. America must lead by deed as well as by example. This is how we plan to lead, and this is the legacy we will leave to those who follow.

www.ingramcontent.com/pod-product-compliance
Lightning Source LLC
Chambersburg PA
CBHW080608290526
45790CB00007B/2685